PRINCEWILL LAGANG

Nurturing Love: A Christian Couple's Devotional

First published by PRINCEWILL LAGANG 2023

Copyright © 2023 by Princewill Lagang

All rights reserved. No part of this publication may be reproduced, stored or transmitted in any form or by any means, electronic, mechanical, photocopying, recording, scanning, or otherwise without written permission from the publisher. It is illegal to copy this book, post it to a website, or distribute it by any other means without permission.

Princewill Lagang asserts the moral right to be identified as the author of this work.

First edition

This book was professionally typeset on Reedsy.
Find out more at reedsy.com

Contents

1	The Foundation of Love	1
2	Communicating with Grace	3
3	Communicating with Grace	5
4	Forgiveness and Reconciliation	7
5	Cultivating Gratitude	10
6	Serving Together with Love	12
7	Overcoming Challenges Together	14
8	Building a Legacy of Love	16
9	The Gift of Intimacy	18
10	A Love That Endures	20
11	A Marriage That Glorifies God	23
12	Pressing Onward Together	25

1

The Foundation of Love

Scripture Passage: 1 Corinthians 13:4-7 (NIV)
> "Love is patient, love is kind. It does not envy, it does not boast, it is not proud. It does not dishonor others, it is not self-seeking, it is not easily angered, it keeps no record of wrongs. Love does not delight in evil but rejoices with the truth. It always protects, always trusts, always hopes, always perseveres."

Reflection:

In the Bible, we find a profound and timeless definition of love in 1 Corinthians 13:4-7. These verses remind us that love is not merely an emotion or a fleeting feeling; it is a deliberate, selfless, and enduring commitment. As we embark on this devotional journey together, it's important to understand that nurturing love in a Christian marriage is about more than just maintaining a romantic connection. It's about building a Christ-centered foundation that can withstand life's challenges and uncertainties.

Questions for Reflection:

1. How do you personally define love in your marriage?
2. In what ways do you see the qualities of patience, kindness, and humility reflected in your relationship?
3. What are some areas in your marriage where you could improve in living out the qualities described in 1 Corinthians 13:4-7?
4. How can you and your spouse work together to build a more Christ-centered foundation for your marriage?

Prayer:

Heavenly Father, we come before you with grateful hearts as we begin this journey to nurture and strengthen our love as a Christian couple. Help us to embody the love described in 1 Corinthians 13:4-7, and may our marriage be a reflection of your love for us. Guide us in building a foundation that is rooted in faith, patience, and selflessness. In Jesus' name, we pray. Amen.

Action Steps:

- Take some time to discuss your answers to the reflection questions with your spouse.
- Make a commitment to read and meditate on 1 Corinthians 13:4-7 regularly throughout this devotional.
- Consider setting aside a specific time for daily or weekly devotionals together to nurture your love and deepen your faith.

2

Communicating with Grace

Scripture Passage: Proverbs 15:1 (NIV)
> "A gentle answer turns away wrath, but a harsh word stirs up anger."

Reflection:

In every Christian marriage, communication plays a pivotal role in nurturing love and building a strong foundation. The words we speak to each other can either strengthen our bond or cause rifts in our relationship. As we continue our journey to deepen our love, we reflect upon Proverbs 15:1, which reminds us of the incredible power of a gentle and gracious response.

Effective communication within a marriage requires more than just words; it demands the art of listening, empathy, and a heart that seeks understanding. In our daily interactions, we have the opportunity to either bless or burden our spouse with our words. The choice between a gentle, loving response and a harsh one often sets the tone for the atmosphere within our home.

Questions for Reflection:

1. Think about a recent interaction with your spouse where communication was challenging. What could you have said or done differently to respond with grace?
2. Reflect on moments in your marriage when communication brought you closer together. What was the key to those positive interactions?
3. Are there recurring issues in your marriage that could be addressed more effectively through grace-filled communication? How can you work together to improve in this area?
4. How can you create an environment of trust and open communication where both you and your spouse feel safe to express your thoughts and feelings?

Prayer:

Heavenly Father, we come before you acknowledging the power of words and the importance of communication in our marriage. Help us, O Lord, to choose our words and responses with grace, that we may bless one another and nurture the love we share. May your wisdom guide us in all our conversations and bring unity to our hearts. In Jesus' name, we pray. Amen.

Action Steps:

- Practice active listening during conversations with your spouse. Avoid interrupting and genuinely seek to understand their perspective.
- Set aside specific times for open and honest communication, where both partners can express their thoughts and feelings without judgment.
- When faced with a disagreement, make a conscious effort to respond with a gentle and grace-filled attitude, rather than reacting in anger or frustration.

3

Communicating with Grace

Scripture Passage: Proverbs 15:1 (NIV)
> "A gentle answer turns away wrath, but a harsh word stirs up anger."

Reflection:

In every Christian marriage, communication plays a pivotal role in nurturing love and building a strong foundation. The words we speak to each other can either strengthen our bond or cause rifts in our relationship. As we continue our journey to deepen our love, we reflect upon Proverbs 15:1, which reminds us of the incredible power of a gentle and gracious response.

Effective communication within a marriage requires more than just words; it demands the art of listening, empathy, and a heart that seeks understanding. In our daily interactions, we have the opportunity to either bless or burden our spouse with our words. The choice between a gentle, loving response and a harsh one often sets the tone for the atmosphere within our home.

Questions for Reflection:

1. Think about a recent interaction with your spouse where communication was challenging. What could you have said or done differently to respond with grace?
2. Reflect on moments in your marriage when communication brought you closer together. What was the key to those positive interactions?
3. Are there recurring issues in your marriage that could be addressed more effectively through grace-filled communication? How can you work together to improve in this area?
4. How can you create an environment of trust and open communication where both you and your spouse feel safe to express your thoughts and feelings?

Prayer:

Heavenly Father, we come before you acknowledging the power of words and the importance of communication in our marriage. Help us, O Lord, to choose our words and responses with grace, that we may bless one another and nurture the love we share. May your wisdom guide us in all our conversations and bring unity to our hearts. In Jesus' name, we pray. Amen.

Action Steps:

- Practice active listening during conversations with your spouse. Avoid interrupting and genuinely seek to understand their perspective.
- Set aside specific times for open and honest communication, where both partners can express their thoughts and feelings without judgment.
- When faced with a disagreement, make a conscious effort to respond with a gentle and grace-filled attitude, rather than reacting in anger or frustration.

4

Forgiveness and Reconciliation

Scripture Passage: Colossians 3:13 (NIV)
> "Bear with each other and forgive one another if any of you has a grievance against someone. Forgive as the Lord forgave you."

Reflection:

In the course of every marriage, misunderstandings and conflicts are inevitable. As we continue our journey to nurture love in our Christian relationship, we confront the significance of forgiveness and reconciliation. Colossians 3:13 calls us to "bear with each other and forgive one another," just as the Lord forgave us.

Forgiveness is a powerful act of love, grace, and humility. It's the willingness to release the hurt, anger, and resentment that can accumulate over time and threaten our connection. When we forgive, we free ourselves and our spouse from the burden of past mistakes, and we open the door to reconciliation and healing.

Remember that forgiveness doesn't mean we condone wrongdoing, but it allows us to seek restoration and renewal in our marriage. By imitating the forgiveness we've received from the Lord, we reflect His love and mercy in our relationship.

Questions for Reflection:

1. Is there a past grievance or issue in your marriage that remains unresolved? How has it affected your relationship?
2. Consider a time when you forgave your spouse. How did forgiveness impact your marriage and your own well-being?
3. Reflect on the way God has forgiven you for your mistakes and shortcomings. How can you extend this grace to your spouse?
4. What steps can you take to facilitate forgiveness and reconciliation in your marriage?

Prayer:

Gracious Lord, we come before you acknowledging our imperfections and the need for forgiveness in our marriage. Help us to forgive one another as you have forgiven us, and grant us the strength to seek reconciliation and healing in our relationship. May our love be a reflection of your boundless grace. In Jesus' name, we pray. Amen.

Action Steps:

- Initiate a loving and honest conversation with your spouse about any unresolved conflicts. Seek to understand each other's perspectives and work towards a resolution.
  - Make a commitment to offer and receive forgiveness freely in your marriage, letting go of grudges and past hurts.
  - Consider reading and discussing a book or resource on forgiveness and reconciliation together to gain insight and tools for managing conflicts in a

healthy way.

5

Cultivating Gratitude

Scripture Passage: 1 Thessalonians 5:18 (NIV)
> "Give thanks in all circumstances; for this is God's will for you in Christ Jesus."

Reflection:

Gratitude is a powerful and transformative force that can deeply impact our marriage and spiritual life. In this chapter, we turn our attention to 1 Thessalonians 5:18, where we are reminded of the divine call to "give thanks in all circumstances." Cultivating gratitude, even in the face of challenges, is a vital aspect of nurturing love in a Christian relationship.

Expressing gratitude towards one another, as well as towards God, fosters an environment of love, joy, and contentment. Gratitude helps us to appreciate the blessings we have, no matter how small, and it allows us to find beauty in the midst of life's struggles. When we are thankful, our hearts are open to the goodness of God, and this, in turn, strengthens our connection with our spouse.

Questions for Reflection:

1. In what ways do you and your spouse currently express gratitude toward each other and God?
2. Reflect on the role of gratitude in your relationship. How has it influenced your love and connection with one another?
3. Are there moments of difficulty or pain in your life where you've struggled to find gratitude? How can you work on cultivating thankfulness in such times?
4. How can you make gratitude a more deliberate and regular practice in your marriage?

Prayer:

Heavenly Father, we come before you with hearts full of gratitude for the love and blessings in our lives. Teach us to be thankful in all circumstances, knowing that this is your will for us. May gratitude be a cornerstone of our relationship, strengthening our bond and drawing us closer to you. In Jesus' name, we pray. Amen.

Action Steps:

- Start a gratitude journal where both you and your spouse can jot down things you are thankful for each day.
  - Create a tradition of sharing moments of gratitude with one another before bedtime or during meals.
  - Make it a practice to thank God for specific blessings in your daily prayers, both individually and as a couple.

6

Serving Together with Love

Scripture Passage: Galatians 5:13 (NIV)
> "You, my brothers and sisters, were called to be free. But do not use your freedom to indulge the flesh; rather, serve one another humbly in love."

Reflection:

Serving one another in love is a fundamental principle in Christian relationships. In Galatians 5:13, we are reminded that our freedom in Christ should be expressed not through self-indulgence but through humble service to our spouse. In this chapter, we explore the concept of serving together with love as a means to nurture our love.

When we serve one another, we emulate Christ's example of humility and selflessness. Service in a marriage involves meeting each other's needs, sometimes before they're even expressed. It's about actively looking for ways to show love and care through small acts of kindness and selfless deeds. As we serve one another, our love grows deeper, and we experience the joy of nurturing a relationship based on mutual respect and love.

SERVING TOGETHER WITH LOVE

Questions for Reflection:

1. In what ways do you currently serve your spouse in your marriage? What is the impact of this service on your relationship?
2. Think about a time when your spouse's selfless service made a significant difference in your day or life. How did it make you feel?
3. Are there areas in your marriage where you could improve in serving one another with love and humility?
4. How can you and your spouse develop a mindset of service as a regular practice in your relationship?

Prayer:

Loving Father, we are grateful for the example of Christ's humble service and the call to serve one another in love. Help us to embrace the spirit of selflessness and find joy in serving our spouse. May our actions reflect your love and strengthen our bond as a couple. In Jesus' name, we pray. Amen.

Action Steps:

- Discuss with your spouse how you can better serve each other, taking note of their preferences and needs.
- Create a list of practical ways to serve one another in your daily lives and agree to actively implement them.
- Make an effort to express appreciation when your spouse serves you, recognizing their acts of love and kindness.

7

Overcoming Challenges Together

Scripture Passage: Romans 8:28 (NIV)
> "And we know that in all things God works for the good of those who love him, who have been called according to his purpose."

Reflection:

In every marriage, challenges and trials are inevitable. It is during these difficult moments that our love is put to the test. In Romans 8:28, we find assurance that God can work all things for the good of those who love Him. In this chapter, we explore the concept of overcoming challenges together as a means to nurture our love.

When we face trials in our marriage, it is an opportunity for growth, both individually and as a couple. Rather than allowing difficulties to drive a wedge between us, we can choose to face them together, leaning on our faith and on each other. In these moments, our love is strengthened, our trust deepens, and our unity grows, as we rely on God's wisdom and grace to guide us through.

Questions for Reflection:

OVERCOMING CHALLENGES TOGETHER

1. Think about a significant challenge or trial you and your spouse have faced in your marriage. How did you overcome it, and what did you learn from the experience?
2. Reflect on how your faith has influenced the way you approach challenges as a couple. In what ways has it provided hope and strength?
3. Are there current challenges in your marriage that you need to confront together? How can you lean on each other and on your faith to overcome them?
4. How can you transform challenges in your marriage into opportunities for growth, rather than viewing them as obstacles?

Prayer:

Heavenly Father, we come before you, acknowledging the difficulties we face in our marriage. We trust that you can work all things for our good, and we ask for the wisdom, strength, and faith to overcome challenges together. Help us to grow closer through trials and to rely on your guidance. In Jesus' name, we pray. Amen.

Action Steps:

- Have an open and honest conversation with your spouse about any current challenges you're facing. Share your feelings and concerns.
- Identify ways you can support each other in facing these challenges. Discuss specific actions you can take together.
- When a challenge is resolved or overcome, take time to celebrate the victory and reflect on the lessons learned.

8

Building a Legacy of Love

Scripture Passage: Proverbs 22:6 (NIV)
> "Start children off on the way they should go, and even when they are old, they will not turn from it."

Reflection:

In every Christian marriage, we have the privilege and responsibility of building a legacy of love that can span generations. Proverbs 22:6 reminds us of the importance of training our children in the ways of the Lord. In this chapter, we explore the concept of building a legacy of love as a means to nurture our own love and faith while leaving a lasting impact on our family.

Our love, faith, and commitment to each other serve as a powerful example to our children and others around us. The way we handle challenges, demonstrate forgiveness, and practice selfless love shapes the values and beliefs of those who look up to us. By intentionally nurturing our love and faith, we can create a legacy that inspires and guides our children and future generations in their own faith and relationships.

Questions for Reflection:

1. How do you and your spouse currently model love and faith for your children or those around you?
2. Reflect on the values and beliefs you wish to pass on to your children and future generations. How can you work on embodying these more effectively?
3. Are there areas in your marriage where you feel you can set a better example for your children or others? How can you improve in these areas?
4. What steps can you take to actively build a legacy of love that reflects your faith and strengthens your marriage?

Prayer:

Heavenly Father, we come before you with a desire to build a legacy of love in our marriage. May our love and faith be a shining example to our children and all those we encounter. Guide us in nurturing our love and passing on the values that honor you. In Jesus' name, we pray. Amen.

Action Steps:

- Have a family meeting with your children, if applicable, to discuss the importance of love, faith, and values in your family.
  - Share stories from your own marriage journey that illustrate important lessons and values.
  - Set aside time for family devotions or discussions about faith and love, involving your children in meaningful conversations.

9

The Gift of Intimacy

Scripture Passage: Song of Solomon 4:7 (NIV)
> "You are altogether beautiful, my darling; there is no flaw in you."

Reflection:

Intimacy in marriage is a precious and sacred gift from God. In the Song of Solomon, we find expressions of love and admiration that reveal the deep emotional and physical connection between two lovers. In this chapter, we explore the concept of intimacy as a means to nurture love in a Christian marriage.

Intimacy involves more than physical closeness; it encompasses emotional, spiritual, and relational aspects as well. It's a place of vulnerability and trust where we can truly be ourselves with our spouse. Intimate moments are opportunities to connect on a deep level, to express love and admiration, and to experience the fullness of the love God designed for marriage. By nurturing intimacy, we can keep the flame of love burning brightly in our relationship.

Questions for Reflection:

1. How do you and your spouse currently experience intimacy in your marriage? What aspects of intimacy are most meaningful to you?
2. Reflect on a time when you felt deeply connected to your spouse on an emotional or spiritual level. What contributed to that experience?
3. Are there any barriers to intimacy in your relationship that you need to address? How can you overcome them?
4. How can you create an environment of trust and vulnerability that fosters intimacy in your marriage?

Prayer:

Heavenly Father, we thank you for the gift of intimacy in marriage. Help us to nurture this sacred connection and draw closer to one another. May our intimacy be a reflection of your love for us and a source of strength for our relationship. In Jesus' name, we pray. Amen.

Action Steps:

- Schedule regular, uninterrupted time for emotional and spiritual connection with your spouse. This could be through deep conversations, shared devotions, or activities that bring you closer.
- Discuss your needs and desires for physical intimacy with your spouse, ensuring that you both feel cherished and fulfilled.
- Make an effort to express love and admiration for your spouse regularly, both in words and actions, to strengthen emotional intimacy.

10

A Love That Endures

Scripture Passage: 1 Corinthians 13:8 (NIV)
> "Love never fails."

Reflection:

In a world marked by change and uncertainty, the enduring love of a Christian marriage is a beacon of hope and stability. In 1 Corinthians 13:8, we are reminded that "love never fails." In this chapter, we explore the concept of a love that endures as the culmination of our journey to nurture love in our relationship.

The love that endures is not based on fleeting emotions, but on a deep commitment and faith in God's design for marriage. It's a love that weathers the storms of life, remains steadfast in adversity, and grows stronger over time. When we cultivate a love that endures, we honor our covenant with God and our spouse, creating a legacy of faithfulness and devotion.

Questions for Reflection:

1. Reflect on the journey of your marriage. In what ways has your love for your spouse endured and grown stronger over time?
2. Consider a challenging period in your marriage. How did your love and faith help you persevere through that difficult time?
3. What are the key ingredients for a love that endures in a Christian marriage? How can you continue to strengthen these aspects in your relationship?
4. How can you ensure that your love remains unwavering in the face of future trials and uncertainties?

Prayer:

Heavenly Father, we thank you for the gift of love that endures. May our marriage be a testament to your unwavering love and faithfulness. Grant us the strength to persevere through life's challenges, always relying on your guidance. In Jesus' name, we pray. Amen.

Action Steps:

- Reflect on the specific ways your love for your spouse has grown stronger over the years, and share these reflections with each other.
- Discuss with your spouse how you can continue to nurture and strengthen your love in the face of future challenges and uncertainties.
- Consider reading a book or resource on the topic of enduring love and commitment in marriage together.

—-

This final chapter serves as a reflection on the enduring love in a Christian marriage, emphasizing the faithfulness, commitment, and steadfastness of love that endures through life's trials and joys. It encourages couples to continually strengthen their love and remain unwavering in their commitment to each other and to God.

11

A Marriage That Glorifies God

Scripture Passage: 1 Corinthians 10:31 (NIV)
> "So whether you eat or drink or whatever you do, do it all for the glory of God."

Reflection:

Our marriage is not just a union of two individuals; it's a covenant that can bring glory to God. In 1 Corinthians 10:31, we're reminded that every aspect of our lives, including our marriage, should be lived in a way that glorifies God. In this chapter, we explore the concept of a marriage that glorifies God as the ultimate purpose of our love and commitment.

A marriage that glorifies God is marked by love, grace, forgiveness, and unity. It's a partnership where both spouses work together to bring God's love and light into their home and the world. When we prioritize God's will and purpose in our marriage, our relationship becomes a beacon of hope and inspiration for others. It's a way to share God's love not just in words but through the example of our love for one another.

Questions for Reflection:

1. Reflect on how your marriage reflects God's love and glory to those around you. What aspects of your relationship do you feel exemplify God's purpose?
2. Are there areas in your marriage where you can improve in bringing glory to God? What changes or actions can you take to align your relationship more closely with God's will?
3. How can your marriage be a source of inspiration and hope for others in your community and beyond?
4. In what ways can you and your spouse actively seek and fulfill God's purpose in your marriage?

Prayer:

Heavenly Father, we come before you with a desire to glorify you through our marriage. May our love, grace, and unity shine as a testimony to your love and purpose in our lives. Guide us in all we do, that our marriage may bring glory to your name. In Jesus' name, we pray. Amen.

Action Steps:

- Discuss with your spouse specific ways you can actively seek and fulfill God's purpose in your marriage, such as by volunteering together or mentoring other couples.
- Set aside time for joint prayer, seeking God's guidance in aligning your marriage more closely with His will.
- Reflect on the impact your marriage has on others, and consider how you can be more intentional about sharing God's love through your relationship.

12

Pressing Onward Together

Scripture Passage: Philippians 3:14 (NIV)
> "I press on toward the goal to win the prize for which God has called me heavenward in Christ Jesus."

Reflection:

In the final chapter of our devotional journey, we reflect on the idea of pressing onward together. The journey of nurturing love in a Christian marriage is ongoing, much like the apostle Paul's pursuit of a higher calling in Philippians 3:14. Our goal is to continue growing in love, faith, and unity as a couple.

As we press onward together, we acknowledge that the journey may have its challenges, but it's in these very moments that we can draw closer to one another and to God. The commitment we've made to nurture our love is not confined to these pages but extends into the everyday journey of our lives together. It's a journey marked by continued growth, deeper faith, and a love that endures through all seasons of life.

Questions for Reflection:

1. Reflect on the progress you've made in nurturing your love throughout this devotional. How has your relationship grown, and in what areas have you seen improvement?
2. What are some specific goals or areas you want to focus on as you press onward in your marriage journey?
3. How can you continue to deepen your faith as a couple, and how can that faith be reflected in your love for each other?
4. How do you envision your marriage in the future, and what steps can you take to make that vision a reality?

Prayer:

Heavenly Father, as we conclude this devotional journey, we thank you for the growth and wisdom we've gained in nurturing our love. Help us to press onward together with faith, love, and unity as we continue our marriage journey. May our relationship be a testimony to your grace and goodness. In Jesus' name, we pray. Amen.

Action Steps:

- Set specific goals for your marriage as you press onward together. These could be related to communication, intimacy, service, or any other aspect you wish to improve.
   - Make a commitment to continue your journey of nurturing love by seeking out additional resources, books, or programs to support your relationship.
   - Share your vision for the future with your spouse and work together to create a plan that aligns with your shared goals.

Book Summary: "Nurturing Love: A Christian Couple's Devotional"

"Nurturing Love: A Christian Couple's Devotional" is a comprehensive guide designed to strengthen the bonds of love and faith within a Christian marriage. With a rich blend of biblical wisdom, practical insights, and thought-provoking questions, this devotional offers couples a roadmap to deepen their connection, nurture their love, and grow together in their walk with Christ.

The devotional is divided into twelve chapters, each dedicated to a specific aspect of fostering a thriving Christian marriage. It begins by emphasizing the importance of a Christ-centered foundation and sets the tone for the journey ahead. Each chapter incorporates a carefully selected scripture passage, providing a spiritual anchor for the theme of the chapter.

Throughout the book, couples are encouraged to engage in meaningful reflection and discussion. Thought-provoking questions prompt couples to consider their individual and shared experiences, fostering open communication and deepening their understanding of each other. Alongside this, each chapter includes prayers and action steps, providing practical ways for couples to put their reflections into practice and actively nurture their love.

Key themes covered in the devotional include building unity through prayer, effective communication, forgiveness and reconciliation, and the power of gratitude. The book also delves into intimacy, the enduring love that withstands trials, and building a legacy of faith and love that can impact generations.

The devotional concludes with a chapter focused on pressing onward together, recognizing that nurturing love is an ongoing journey. It encourages couples to set new goals and continue deepening their faith, love, and unity in their shared path of life.

"Nurturing Love: A Christian Couple's Devotional" is a valuable resource for Christian couples at any stage of their relationship. It inspires them to prioritize their love and faith, ultimately allowing their marriage to serve as a testimony of God's grace and a source of inspiration for others. This devotional is not just a book to read, but a guide to living out a faith-filled and love-centered marriage.

www.ingramcontent.com/pod-product-compliance
Lightning Source LLC
LaVergne TN
LVHW020740090526
838202LV00057BA/6148